D1582842

HIGHGATE MUMS

HIGHGATE MUMS

OVERHEARD WISDOM FROM THE LADIES WHO BRUNCH

DAN HALL

Atlantic Books
LONDON

First published in hardback in Great Britain in 2016 by Atlantic Books, an imprint of Atlantic Books Ltd.

A catalogue record for this book is available from the British Library.

Hardback: 978-1-78649-076-6
E-book: 978-1-78649-077-3

Highgate Mums is a registered trade mark of Dan Hall.

Every effort has been made to credit authors of tweets. Please contact the publishers with any corrections.

Designed and typeset by Dan Mogford
Illustrations by Dan Mogford and Freepik
Printed in Italy by 🐢 Grafica Veneta S.p.A.

Atlantic Books
An Imprint of Atlantic Books Ltd
Ormond House
26–27 Boswell Street
London

www.atlantic-books.co.uk

CONTENTS

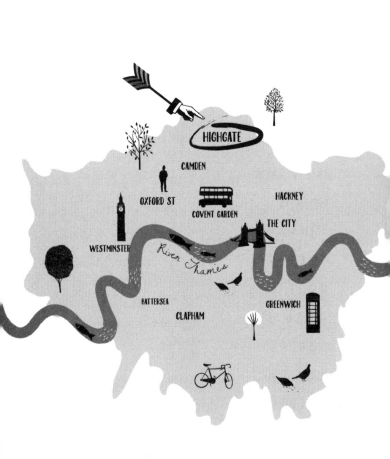

HIGHGATE

CAMDEN

OXFORD ST

WESTMINSTER

COVENT GARDEN

HACKNEY

THE CITY

River Thames

BATTERSEA

CLAPHAM

GREENWICH

INTRODUCTION

Don't be fooled into thinking Highgate Mums (HM) has much to do with Highgate, or indeed mums. In a recent straw poll I asked whether our heroes could be found in other parts of London. The answers came speedily: Putney, Earlsfield, Dulwich, Balham, Notting Hill and Barnes ('If you don't own a child there's an actual law to prevent you living there').

Then the London portion of my question fell by the wayside, quickly yielding:

- Cotswold-ville – Tetbury or Chipping Camden
- Harrogate ('from one end to the other')
- West End of Glasgow ('although maybe not so much now the Steiner School's burnt down')
- Roath and Cathays, Cardiff
- Most of Bristol
- Chiswick and Guilford
- Jesmond in Newcastle (rich students 'slumming it up North but at least there's a Waitrose')
- Deansgate, Manchester
- Cobham, Weybridge and Esher

And then the responses went wonderfully global:
- Hong Kong ('full of tai tai mums who don't work, drink coffee and complain about their Amah maids wanting a day off every month!')
- Ninety percent of Los Angeles
- 'Don't even get me started #Singapore'
- 'Duuuuuude. PERTH. So. Much. Perth.' (Australia)
- Brooklyn ('Williamsburg to be precise.') (New York, America)
- The whole of Melbourne. (Australia)
- 'Posh Potomac' (Maryland, America).

So it was true! The unique breed of HM was not so unique after all. It wasn't unique to London, to the South, to England or even to Europe. The HMs and their massive buggies were everywhere. And we loved it.

When HM first began we were accused of finger-pointing and bordering on misogynistic. It's an accusation that I found hard to disagree with. But something wonderful happened. Once we hit about 7,000 followers the expression 'Highgate Mum' stopped being about mocking the Other, and began to be used just as much as an adjective to laugh about oneself. Followers announced with shame their HM moments, or reported their kids and friends.

This delighted me and gave HM a kindness that I felt was lacking in many of the other overhear accounts that run on Twitter. We were appalled and disgusted, but if we were honest we saw more than a fleeting shadow of ourselves. It reminded me of a poster for *Star Wars: Episode I* in which a boy,

Anakin Skywalker, walks through the desert, his cast shadow showing the unmistakable form of the adult Darth Vader that he would become. Laugh at the silliness, the selfishness and the peculiar narrow-mindedness, but when you find yourself sneering, look at your shadow and you'll see a huge shoulder bag and a buggy the size of Westminster Tube station.

During the writing of this book, the attack took place on the world's LGBTI community at The Pulse nightclub in Orlando. In the immediate aftermath Dan Savage spoke movingly on his *Savage Lovecast* podcast. I'd like to thank him for helping to ease sadness and anger. From a stranger across the ocean, to all of you affected, I send utmost love.

What this book doesn't contain (because it's not funny) are the moments when the HM proved themselves fantastic. After the Paris shootings in 2015 there were discussions about changing holiday plans and visiting Paris instead to show their support. They can't abide Katie Hopkins or her politics, and as a gay man I've applauded their apparent total support for gay marriage. This isn't the stuff of comedy quips on Twitter, but is a key part of the HM psyche. And they should rightfully be applauded.

There's many people to thank for encouraging HM. My lovely extended family (Guy, Sam, Jo, Jamie, Issy, Evye, Jollie and Marcus) and my ever-loyal flatmate and pup, Moray Laing. There are also the wonderful early adopters Wendy Gordon, Elaine Blanchard, Morwenna Lawson, Lisa Shearon, Pablo Muñoz, Catherine Catton, Rebecca Parker, Tash Baylis, Glen 'Bruce' Oldershaw and

Johann Knobel. It was they who initially persuaded the over-hears to be taken from the privacy of Facebook and into the public realm of Twitter thanks to this tweet:

'The problem with poor people is they don't realise chorizo sausages are better value than sausage rolls'.

I'd heard this in a café up in Highgate Village, a leafy and pretty area of North London where I lived. The group was a team of mums sat at a round table having an excited and friendly discussion about the ongoing recession. But there was was one voice that I noticed above all others, which was steadily growing louder. 'The problem, the PROB-lem, THE PROBLEM...' she persisted until she had everyone's attention, and then the above about chorizo was delivered to silence, except for the squeak of a rocking buggy.

Within five minutes @Highgatemums had been registered, and friend and broadcaster Zeb Soanes suggested the fantastic tagline: 'Overheard words of wisdom from the ladies who brunch'.

I have never publicized the account. Across five years the rise on Twitter from zero to over 45,000 followers (at the time of writing) is purely due to word-of-mouth. To those people who cheered, re-tweeted and pulled in more followers I also offer a big thank you.

At intervals I am accused of making these up. And to some extent that's true. Few of the quotes in this collection came out of mouths as perfectly formed tweets. Rather they're paraphrased content taken from longer statements or general conversations condensed into bite-sized ideologies. But the listens, the moods, the lattes are all very real. And how do I know? Because I love coffee life. I love cafés. Best of all, I love being an appalling hypocrite.

A big professional thank you to the team at Atlantic Books for showing faith in the project. And to my main man at Atlantic – James Nightingale – who has been a brilliant editor and ambassador since day one. To Stephen Emms and Tom Kihl at London Belongs To Me who were instrumental in building North London momentum behind the project via their fantastic newspaper *Kentishtowner*. And finally to my literary agent David Luxton and published author chums Richard Moore and Patrick Gale, who have always been on-hand to help me through the unknown world of book publishing.

If you want to go on your own HM safari, you could do worse than visiting Bread and Bean (37 Junction Road, London N19 5QU) or The Spoke (710 Holloway Road, London N19 3NH). Both are dangerously close to the nearby Montessori school and provide a delightful seam of chatter. More importantly, they also serve the best coffee in North London. There's also Côte Brasserie, Caffè Nero and Le Pain Quotidien on Highgate High Street. All these places have been at the heart of inspiring this book.

And a final thanks to my very own Highgate Mum, Sue Hall. In so many ways she brought me here in the first place. Thanks, Mum!

DAN HALL, JULY 2016

FOOD & DRINK

'Well, porridge can be for anyone. Not just the poor.'

Although the posts of others form the backbone of the HM Twitter account, not everything gets a retweet. This category flags the most 'faker!' klaxons when my editor's eyes look at the list on our feed. I'm often sent cut-and-paste apparent overhears regarding kids with silly names complaining about extra virgin olive oil or some obscure fruit from Venezuela. The HM is far beyond such transparent social superficiality, as cited recently by a smart mum saying with a sad sigh:

'Specialist oils are as common as Corn Flakes now.'

What are the expectations of the HM kitchen table? For there is arguably no better place than this to showcase the effortless delight of a simple and sophisticated life:

I spilt chia seeds all over the breakfast bar this morning. That stuff gets everywhere. (@mango_ruby)

'Pesto's no fun since fresh basil became so affordable.'

I've just been offered an 'artisan crouton' in a restaurant. (@Sparklyboy1)

'... just a quick homemade snack of a lime crush blend and fresh chilli-roasted nuts.'

'My... I just LOVE heritage tomatoes.'

We have to bow to Food & Drink, as the chorizo overhear (see Introduction) was where it all started. And the needs of a TV-lifestyle kitchen (without, of course, a TV) means the HM-isms of the household are quickly absorbed by the young:

My seven-year-old (Hampstead) son tells me: 'The teachers asked how they could improve school dinners. I said "king prawns".' (@debstewart)

'Mum can you not put so much algae in my smoothie, it tastes of Japan.' (@LadyKilligrew)

Tesco, Highgate. Child aged about four: 'Daddy, I can't find the risotto rice.'

In Cotswold pub offering complimentary cucumber and mint water, my nine-year-old, 'It tastes like drinking Tzatziki!' (@CotswoldVillan)

On the Tube, my almost three-year-old, 'What's that lady eating? Maybe it's goji berries!' (@cathredfern)

'That guacamole looks good.' 'It's mushy peas, darling.' (@stuartctaylor)

Occasionally, the true dining desires of the kids seep out. The devil inside their impish little souls escapes, dreaming of Monster Munch and boiled sweets with the flavour of petrochemical factories. But brand HM is ever-present to snap things back into place:

Portsmouth train to London, 'Mummy, can I have a biscuit?' 'They're oatcakes, darling.' (@KCMANC)

'No, Darling. Don't pick from the *Prix Fixe*. Those dishes are always full of fat.'

'We've been OVER this. You KNOW how to take the pips out of grapes.'

'If you change your dairy to soya I'll let you have a pastry.'

'Don't tear the croissant with your teeth, darling. Tear a bit off like this.'

Leaving the safety of home can be treacherous as caring eyes are no longer able to scrutinise raw ingredients. Who knows what acerbic cleaning materials have been used in restaurant dishwashers? Or one's vital – possibly FATAL – need to avoid wheat? It's comforting therefore to see that serving staff (like teachers – see Chapter Two) know their place:

A woman in Starbucks just asked for room temperature water... At the request of her seven or eight-year-old daughter. (@Bradleyzread)

(to waitress) 'What types of fresh black pepper do you have?'

'Is the hot chocolate cocoa-heavy, or does it tinge towards the sugared and the saccharine?'

'No, Milo. Lollipops are for aeroplanes, darling. You can have some edamame instead.' (@1scrummymummy)

(ordering) '... and the poached eggs with soldiers. But could she have toast and bread soldiers laid out alternately.'

(girl, about eight, to barista) 'I only want a brownie if it's horse-coloured. I don't WANT THOSE ONES.'

'Would you mind turning off the music so my daughter can sleep?'

Me to 4-year-old in cafe: 'Would you like some of this cake?' 4-year-old: 'No Mummy, I'd rather have that baklava.' (@phanellafine)

'Do you have any sort of flatbread for kids?'

Cafe in Tufnell Park: Savannah, the six-year-old vegetarian, only wants avocado on toast if it's organic. (@SianySianySiany)

Sometimes kids are complaining or longing for things that are a mystery to me. But with impeccable taste developed from the nipple, is it any wonder that they'd shame even the palate of delicious local Giles Coren:

Was laughing at @Highgatemums until my mum reminded me I used to take bok choi and smoked mackerel for my packed lunch in primary school.

Five-year-old eating an old school iced bun, 'Mummy, this brioche with icing is lovely.'

My 10-year-old just moaned because we have no brie in the fridge at our caravan. (@fifi_manson)

Child playing at mine (SW London) when I offered her kiwi: 'Is it GOLDEN kiwi?' (@PetrovaFossil71)

Four-year-old sister just asked for olive oil on her salad. Thought of you immediately. (@BenSadler17)

'Mummy, Ribena tastes different when it's in a plastic cup, doesn't it?'

My four-year-old daughter, whilst eating Haribos: 'Daddy, this one tastes of papaya.' (@rulitos14)

With the HM dinner table inspiring the child to try the best food that money can buy, it comes as no surprise that their foodie light shines bright, even away from the home:

'There is far too much truffle oil on my pizza'
(@charliestarlie)

Did HM have a trip to Foyles today? Eight-year-old boy in the cafe: 'Mummy, what's the best country for *white* wine?' (@vicky_walker)

'Excuse me? Excuse me? Hello? Yes, please could I have this babycino heated up? It's a dash too tepid.' #lattedad

Children at Sainsbury's overheard discussing relative merits between Pad Thai or Udon noodles. (@Bernard_Collier)

Kid in Waitrose, looking at a display of plums, 'Mummy, are these damsons?' (@trellism)

Our two-year-old when given a breadstick to avoid hunger tantrum in car: 'Where's the hummus?' We have joined the ranks of HM. (@MrAColley)

With my six-year-old daughter in McDonalds, she asked for sparkling Elderflower as her Happy Meal. (@katstheone)

Kids telling me about the balsamic vinegar at school dinners. 'You can put it on your bread.' (@wotclaire)

I'm never short of food reports from our followers, and this set below are a bunch that have tickled me when compiling this book:

Berkshire child, 'There is a fantastic Waitrose next door. They sell dried mango.' (Tash, friend)

Eight-year-old in small pub in Devon, 'Could I please have a gingerbread latte?' (@MaddyHowlter)

Daughter asked favourite sandwich filling by violin teacher, replies 'Smoked salmon'. (@craggyliz)

ME: 'I'm off to the supermarket, any requests?' 5-YEAR-OLD: I'd like brioche, mummy.' (@Annabel_C_Price)

But it is when we catch ourselves or our friends that the seam of HM is at its most pure. Those beautiful moments of self-realisation, and forehead-slapping:

The other day I was screaming, 'I just can't find a fucking croissant for Eddie anywhere on the high street!' (Gennie, friend)

I found myself saying, 'When we order-in oriental takeaway an Arab-type man delivers it. That doesn't do anything for the Asian experience.' (anon)

HM, My friend just became middle class, 'I finish in an hour and I'm dreaming of pesto and calzone, and prosecco of course.' (@Ad_Smart)

I snapped at my son in Le Pain Quotidien, 'Darling, darling, darling. Just chose from the pastries. Don't digress to savouries.' (anon)

Stood in Waitrose, just heard myself thinking, 'Well this is a very disappointing selection of granola.' (@bodhmall)

And being the coffee snob that I am, I absolutely agree with this:

'I won't drink a coffee anywhere that serves syrup.'

And this chapter comes to a close in The Spoke on Holloway Road, with its rusted, reclaimed furniture taken from what appears to be a school. As a reward breakfast shall be ordered, likely 'Polly's Porridge'. And while I shamefully enjoy the 'fresh fruit, cinnamon and almond flakes' that come with it, I'll munch away happy that this poshed-up peasants' food is being served in a cafe that's a million times nicer than the smoky shithole of a pub that was previously on this spot.

EDUCATION

'We're paymasters to the teachers and guardians to the kids. It's about time they remembered that. ALL of them!'

The war zones of the world have nothing on the politics and posturing in the HM education system. There is a constant disappointment at the quality of service delivered by teachers and pupils alike:

'With teachers you're dealing with a second or sometimes at best third-rate version of yourself.'

It is a most perfect foil against which the HM can protect their brand: a failing teacher is responsible for an underperforming child; a disruptive child cannot be held accountable for lessons that don't engage them. And all the time the HM rests regal, knowing that grades would have been just that bit better if only everyone else had listened to them:

'The trust of the parent is far more important than that of the pupil.'

'I'm frankly aghast at the school's inability to think first of parents.'

'No thought is ever given in the curriculum for us.'

'I've learned that you need to see the bad in every school in order to push them to the next level. It's vital. See ONLY the bad.'

These overhears tend to come in clusters. A local teacher and friend noticed that these outbursts come at the first coffee of term, or the morning after Parents' Evening. The HM brand is under attack from teachers, pupils, the government. And the defensive roars begin:

'I'm hauled in regularly about her behaviour, as if I'm somehow responsible!'

'Yes, mine's in the lowest tier, but I'm convinced she's being used to be an aspirational focus for her less-abled classmates.'

'I'll get my girls as quickly and safely as I can to the school gate, but if North Road is blocked WHAT - CAN - I DO?'

'My kids are horribly influenced by the playground. The latest is wanting to watch TELEVISION.'

'And her bedroom. Her BEDROOM! Since she met those Finchley girls, everything is posters and pop culture... and all of it in English.'

'Okay, hands up – MY FAULT! Yes, for wanting my girls to be wanted in the employment market. Not having to beg in bloody job interviews.'

'The teaching staff act like they're in charge.'

The fire and fury against those in loco parentis is outside of reason and sense. From what I hear all underperformance is the fault of teachers, other (possible fat) pupils or an inability to understand that the entire education system is there to service the one child:

'Who can blame her for being a bit of a bitch? Cause and effect, even in the classroom. Teachers aren't gods and shouldn't behave as such.'

'How much do teachers earn? And they expect their pupils to respect them?!'

'It would help to diffuse arguments if they put more points in for the girls to charge their phones.'

'Their English teacher massively overrates Iris Murdoch. At the expense of my-heart-bleeds-to-dread what else.'

'Is it so wrong to see a teacher/child parity? One has no more right to discipline than the other.'

'All teachers do is spout out stuff they already know. It's our daughters who are having to learn.'

'He's a fantastic teacher. He knows his authority but also his place.'

I danced through the education system through the 1980s. We made friends and enemies to gain access to scented rubbers (erasers) and Nintendo Game & Watch. Whiteboards were magical tech, held only by the higher-funded science departments. Not wishing to sound like an old fart, these palaces of learning today sound like a bloody Apple store:

'Having daylight bulbs in the classroom would surely lift them out of apathy.'

'The kids are furious. At lunchtime the Wi-Fi is so overloaded it's impossible to access YouTube.'

'Those corridors are un-inspiringly dim once the sun has passed midday.'

'They have sourdough to make the school dinners seem classy, but ruin it by making the kids eat with IKEA cutlery. A waste of time!'

'The work is not getting the council to paint the common room, but in getting them to do it to a finish that we would expect.'

And even within the system itself I suspect my own learning would be utterly useless. While I was a toddler my tiny brain was too easily satisfied with finger-painting and eating the corners of Mr Men books. I shudder to wonder what learning milestones are in place today. And wow… who takes the credit for them?

12yo son: 'Got a drama test today.' Me: 'What are they testing you on?' 12yo son: 'Commedia dell'arte.' (@The_MadriGals)

'I'm not sure the classroom concept ever quite works for our daughters.'

'We like to think it's beyond education. More thought-construction.'

Overheard in Kensington - child 1 to child 2: 'I'm sure you'll be an excellent ambassador for Further Maths.' (@tiganajbitch)

'If the school won't let me take him out for holidays when I like that's crazy. He's three now and can read and write and has the vocab of six-year-old!'

'They don't want us going into the Chemistry lab because some of the equipment has been recycled from two, even three years ago.'

'EVERYTHING they know about sex these days is from those awful white girls singing with Cockney accents.'

And with such standards, is it any surprise that the children themselves are a quivering disappointment? Watch them roam Highgate High Street, eyes wide with fear. Those gym-obsessed seventeen-year-old boys and lanky-legged girls in tiny skirts, all worrying about Anna Akhmatova. In fact, they should be getting off down Highgate's alleyways, lit only by period faux-gas lamps that were passionately fought for by the local preservation society. I'm not sure the teens have it as easy as we might imagine:

'Jessica! If you don't learn to spell your teacher will think you're just like the rest of them.'

'You've got to focus on teenage to-do lists or they end up like they're bloody fathers.'

'Her and her friends all get together. They're so loud. And they have no appreciation for ANYTHING.' (The irony lost)

And god help this lad:

'I had to have a talk with him about the masturbation.'

But at least the younger ones don't escape either:

'I had to point out to Head of Year 5 that my boy's "dyslexia" means nothing to a headhunter with a pile of CVs.'

Heard in Hampshire today. To a three or four-year-old child: 'Well, you don't HAVE to go to university, darling.' (@tabby_whisperer)

'Don't be upset, darling. In any concrete jungle there's going to be beautiful trees that put all the other girls in the shade.'

But amongst all the trauma and let-down, it's good to hear that the school is not primarily a place of education. Not AT ALL.

'That teacher fails to give the class any sense of brand or identity within the school.'

Picked up an entry form for PTA quiz night. You can pre-order bottles of Merlot, Rioja, Sauvignon Blanc and Prosecco. (@jezhiggins)

Every day of every week the (mostly private) education system lists and threatens to sink. Its ballast is overwhelmed with the demands of the National Curriculum (boo, hiss!) and the union-bullying need for teachers to have weekends ('why should they when we don't?'). But despite these cesspits of incompetence, at least it's not State.

'Surely there's some sort of Parent's Evening where we have a forum to report back to the teachers on their work?'

'Here in Hereford, a local academy-status primary school is having an ice rink at its Christmas fair. My kid's has a bran tub.' (@JudSawyer)

'Can someone work out some sort of efficiency chart to make sure the staff are doing what they're supposed to?'

'Teachers with tattoos should wear long sleeves. Even in comprehensives.'

'What leads someone to want to become a teacher? I never know how much of it is choice.'

'Teachers are creatures of habit.'

'The difference between State and Private is the pitter-patter of self-respect.'

My Finchley comprehensive school education clearly wasn't smart enough. I've had to look up 'Commedia dell'arte', I don't know what a 'bran tub' is and I have absolutely no idea what the difference in taste is between Merlot and Rioja (my option at the table would be to go for whichever is the cheaper). But boy, these schools sound like an exhausting place to be;

for the teachers, the parents and the poor bloody kids at the heart of it all.

But if you arrive at the right time of day, you see kids in Caffè Nero ignoring their iPads and instead trying to play with the free toy from a magazine. And while the parents are pouring over a choice of pastries, you'll notice stolen teen glances across the room. It's a relief to know that despite everything, despite the fees, the pushy parenting, that those teens are actually just thinking about that alleyway near to The Wrestlers pub where the CCTV broke last week and the faux-gas streetlight shines a beam bright enough to see, and dim enough to hide.

ASPIRATION

Showing Mum @Highgatemums and she reminds me how at four years old I told the harvest service that my favourite cheese was camembert.

Aspiration – the curse of the human condition. It's the reaching for something, *anything*, that signifies a move forward. First it's a utility room, then it's two, then there's no room to store the ski equipment so a basement is needed. How keen we all are to show the world what we think we're worth. Or even better, to have others remind us:

Overheard in dentists: 'Yes, Daddy is a Brigadier. But then nearly everyone you meet is a Brigadier, or will be soon.' (@larkrise2candle)

Overheard woman on phone whispering, 'I'm in a supermarket'. Something is said to which she exclaims loudly 'No! WAITROSE!' (@Becks01483)

Overheard this morning 'civilisation basically ends at Parsons Green'. (@_dreamfunda)

Drinking decaf Earl Grey from a handcrafted ceramic mug made by my friend's grandmother. Feeling agonisingly HM. (@maryjayneagain)

For my 21st birthday my husband got me a wine decanter. I'm pretty sure i'm fast approaching HM territory. (@shutup_maria)

'It's not a jacket, mummy, it's a gilet.' (@honoroakhill)

I once loudly asked my 5-yr-old, in Guggenheim, Venice 'Who do you think that's by, darling?'. I knew she'd say Picasso. (@MichelleLGa)

Overheard loud parenting on the Penzance to Paddington train, getting two-year-old to do phonics for benefit of commuters. (@emilythecat)

Kids are an aspirational pain. They are your path to enlightenment, whilst simultaneously being responsible usually for your exclusion. They have no idea the EFFORT and AGONY required to lifestyle more than just a job-lot of Sally Bourne cast-offs.

'Sweetheart, I don't blame the art teacher for scolding you. This piece is devastatingly lacklustre.'

Me: 'Where shall we go for lunch after the Ballet on Saturday?' Him: 'Burger King?' Class act my kid. Totes debunked my pseudo-HM status. (@KjDouglas)

Overheard today, said to a 4-year-old, 'Until you know how to spell Valkyrie you'll never get anywhere in life.' (@Lou_Roll)

Overheard on Southwest Trains mum to 10-year-old 'and that's why you need to go to university. So you don't become a bog cleaner.' (@chvrlee)

Heard in Waitrose car park, 'Put that carrier bag back in the boot. We can't use a Tesco bag in there.' (@au_somemum)

Turning myself in: Child 'Beans beans they make you far' Me 'It's farT. There's a T on the end.' (@SheyMouse)

Overheard at Asda, 'Oh that's terribly common, we could just cover up the print.' In reference to a child's *Frozen* dress. (@TitchyMixz)

WAITROSE

But sometimes they make you proud:

A 7-year-old, 'My hobbies are maths, art and Paris.' (@iraturkey)

My 14-year-old son asking me if I knew where he could buy a reclaimed mango wood wardrobe for his bedroom. (@ColinC34)

Six-year-old on her way to school in Exeter, 'So daddy, how many years study is a PhD?' (@emilythecat)

Two six-year-olds role playing. 'Let's make a shop' 'Yes! It could be John Lewis!' (@MrsHodge1978)

'Her first words were "shoes" and "brioche".'

Amazing HM moment in Crouch End, six-year-old old to mum, 'I hope the old KFC becomes a new Whole Foods shop.'

It's a blessing that the ever-powerful world of retail is there to help guide the squawking tots in the right direction:

'Posh wine shop down the road is hosting a lunchtime "Mothers and Babies Chenin Blanc tasting".' (@Pollylwh)

'I can't stand a café with a community board. Thank God there's none around here.'

'**And Asda is what keeps the even riff-ier raff away from Sainsbury's**' (@Cal_Lad85)

'**They let her enter my PIN number. It's an absolute hoot. And a highlight for the barista girl.**'

I visited a restaurant that had a salmon, kale and pesto dish on the children's menu today. (@CharlotteKaye)

I may have reached peak middle class. Had fish and chips with the in-laws and they'd laid out FISH KNIVES. Sweet baby Jesus. (@mim_monk)

The HM are appallingly mischievous at feeding each other's aspirations. Conversations swirl around material stuff: holidays, excellent grades or a rare yoga teacher that nobody has yet discovered. Achievements are delicately dropped into conversation so as not to appear boastful, but done with enough force so as to make their message most perfectly heard:

'**Is it normal to do that? ... Oh, I just wondered. Mine doesn't ... But then again, mine's talking now so there it is.**'

'**It's absolutely ridiculous that I should be expected to work.**'

Overheard once sat by the river, 'It's the worst barn conversion we've ever lived in.' (@janmorgan8)

'We discourage them from listening to pop records. The form is too simplistic.'

'The baking space isn't really a separate kitchen. Not as I see it. But it does help to keep the main one tidy.'

Who's going to make me a Christmas cake so I can pretend my kid made it for the cake sale? (@elianas_world)

But STOP THERE! Don't think that the kids aren't also possessed. Back in my teen days we fled to Camden Town to get away from materialism and aspiration. Now they run there to find it. And the younger ones? I'm suspecting that your sibling's Lego and a circular bit of Hornby model railway won't make the grade any longer:

A 6-year-old to another in a tennis lesson today: 'Excuses stop you from achieving what you want.' #LifeLessons (@biscuitchaser)

Overheard two five-year-olds, 'I'm going to be a solicitor or a YouTuber, which one do you think's easier?' #moderncareers (@jofflean)

We had a magic flying suitcase this week. I asked the two Four-year-olds where they wanted it to take us. 'Antigua'... (@Debutots_Jen)

Today's gem from my 9-year-old. Sat in a tea room, 'Daddy is this fair trade hot chocolate?' What have I created? (@woody_2k)

To bed, rain hammering down. Daughter number one debating Sylvia Path/Ted Hughes, number two wanting to learn more German. (@MichelleLGa)

In Amsterdam, my 5-year-old, 'I played painters in the playground. I was Van Gogh and my friend was Rembrandt.'

When my youngest was three she kept asking for 'poco shon-alan'. Finally realised she wanted: pain aux chocolat. (@StaticKing)

Adult to child in Hampstead park sandpit: 'What's that you're making, is it a mud pie?' Child: 'No, it's a wild boar pie.'

And me? Well I'm writing this chapter at the Balans Soho Society in Central London, early before heading to the day job. I'm here because the coffee is good and they play sassy early Motown in the mornings. Oh, and because the walls are painted the same Sally Bourne Interiors slate grey that I've earmarked for my new front door. It'll be one of the first in the street, and I know it's quite the statement.

Hedge Fund Grey

THE CHILDREN

> 'Everyone's having children these days. There'll be no room anywhere for those of us that got there first.'

Arguably the only thing worse than childless people are those with children. Because the tots of others are appalling, rude, out of control and bordering on the mentally ill. The HM has no time for them, except as examples to show how excellent their own parenting and children are:

'The discipline amongst those girls is shocking. And I'd know. I visited Yugoslavia during the war.'

'Absolutely, I'm partisan. But she speaks rubbish. I don't like her. And my daughter says her children are appalling in class.'

'Oh, I can't stand Petersham Nurseries. It's full of loud parents with spoiled children.'

But of course, the behaviour of one's own children is not appalling at all. And should be carved into natural waxed oak tablets as a touchstone for others:

'Why should a child be forced to apologise if they find it humiliating?'

'Who cares about tantrums or crying? If you love a child, everything it does is a joy.'

'You can't deny that a child, regardless of age, should not be allowed prolonged frustration.'

'Why should I tell her to stop singing? A coffee shop is a public place.'

'Thankfully there is no end to a child's capacity to make its message heard.'

'We try not to undermine Kirwin's winning mindset by pressuring him to appear gracious.' (@NinerRobSFO)

(in a cafe, to child) 'Make some crumbs and put them in a pretty pattern.'

But is it any wonder the HM feel so threatened by the children of others? These tiny socialites have aspirations way beyond my own, and a focus on lifestyle that blows mine out of the water:

Aghast. Daughter (two-and-a-half years old) asked husband at bedtime this eve, 'Daddy, what's a Buche de Noel?' HM Level Ten: COMPLETE. (@Tootingbaby)

My three-year-old just announced in Aldi that he'd like dressed crab for his lunch. (@beckyuk)

In our house today, Mum: Salmon bagels for lunch. Five-year-old reply: Have you got any dill? (@clucks)

Children report in casual tones that they had foie gras and game casserole for lunch. (@ginandting)

(HM to toddler in buggy) 'They don't have the sushi you like, darling – can you bear to try a different one?' (@zvjlawrence)

My eight-year-old son talking to friends, 'My favourite ice cream flavour is salted caramel with peanuts.' (@fionamocatta)

Me: Would you like one of these little biscuits? Five-year-old boy: They're called macaroons. (@SamanthaNevill5)

However, with the prodigy status comes the inevitable tantrums and fury. And the HM must be forced to deal with this in a day's work:

(child, about six years old) 'I can't be expected to live like this.'

'You're in my mind and IT'S VEXING ME.' (teen to HM)

Christmas meltdown from our four-year-old because the honey wasn't 'Manuka'. (@Toriatastic76)

'I'm two steps from walking out!' (approx. six-year-old)

(child about eight years old) 'I don't want a pain au raisin, I WANT an almond croissant.'

(child about seven years old) 'Mummy, sometimes I feel like I don't belong in this family.'

'I bet you wouldn't treat Dad like this.' (furious and clearly very spoilt teenager)

And praise God that the discipline is swift and effective:

'Darling, don't scrape your chair. It makes your presence over-known.'

'Close your mouth, darling, no one wants to see your masticated food.' (@maccagraeme)

'It's not a nasty thing, she just feels threatened by people on the Victoria Line.'

VICTORIA LINE

'Stop that! Or everyone at the table will think less of you.' (to young child)

'They reward and punish with hugs. A punish hug lasts only two seconds. But it's what they call loving discipline.'

My eight-year-old grandson has started a poetry blog.
(@GazWeetman)

The never-ending danger of living is a huge worry for the HM and in the wrong mood they can get shockingly defensive:

'I think it's perfectly fair to be suspicious of any man over 30 who doesn't have an up-to-date CRB check.'

'Who cares about sacrificing freedoms if it makes children safer? Who could possibly argue against it?'

'Surely the caretaker doesn't have to be on-site when the girls are there.'

'The safety of children must be paramount over all other things and freedoms.'

Kept free from the sharp edges of life, we are left with a beautifully mannered brood, ready to step into the sun and become the next generation of all things pain aux raisins:

Just heard a child address its mother as 'Mamma' with the emphasis on the 2nd syllable. In 2014. In SE London. (@AnnaA77)

(on bus) 'Mummy, can you tell those people to move off my favourite seat?'

Mum: 'You can't have a biscuit now, not until we get home.' Kid: 'I am very disappointed in you.' (@NotRollergirl)

Three-year-old on the Tube, 'Mummy I want a massage.' (@victoriajayco)

'He doesn't like sharing buses with other passengers.'

In true HM style, today we are off to a museum then John Lewis for lunch as chosen by my five-year-old. (@MrsHodge1978)

Small they may be, but these kids have a keen eye on modern society. Often the nail is hit with surprising accuracy:

'Alan Sugar's suit looks like it's from a shop. Bet he's smiling because he's a Lord.' (child in Waterstones, Hampstead)

My own son – nine – visiting Blackheath, 'Mummy, it's just like Hampstead, there's a Farrow & Ball.' (@nat_balance)

But please do remember, that as confident as they may seem, they are so very, very, very, VERY vulnerable. For heaven's sake, WON'T SOMEBODY THINK OF THE CHILDREN?

Child (circa ten-year-old) in Kensington, crying as if the world were ending: 'NO, mummy! I wanted TRIANGLE diamonds!' (@_scarscarscar_)

'I think it intimidates the children if teachers live in the area where they work.'

A mum in my pub told us we should have toys for the children... It's a pub. (@moolaboo)

'I'm just not comfortable with a man being alone in a classroom containing my daughter. Not comfortable AT ALL.'

(to cafe owner) 'Can you turn the heating up? My daughter said she's feeling cold.'

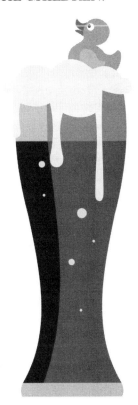

And my favourite:

> **'Graduates who have degrees are forced to work in pubs these days.'**

It is not unnoticed by me that arguably this chapter has absolutely no right to be here. As a single man without kids I don't have a good idea of the challenges faced by HM. In the 1990s my pal Megan introduced me to Magic Sea Horses. This powder was poured into a small plastic tub and – WOW! – suddenly little living creatures appeared out of suspended animation. These little things were in my care. These were living things!

By the weekend they were all dead.

But in order to save people like me from becoming nasty, grouchy old bastards, I pray to HM to please stop offering food choices to your kids. It makes them infinitely dissatisfied. Trust me, they don't really care whether it's a croissant or a peach-stuffed pastry. Because they'll take a few bites, make crumbs into the shape of Norway and drop the rest into my computer bag.

NEWS & CONFLICT

In A&E with a knife wound. Reception: Was it a fight? Me: Good lord, no — I was slicing an avocado. (@RichHawkins)

News is, of course, where it's at. In the tenseness of conflict and warfare the naked truths of humanity are revealed. And in the streets and cafes of N6 (and increasingly N19) conflict is fascinating as it often challenges the kindness of manners. The HM may be many things, but she is not malicious. So what on earth is the mild, polite, well-bred HM to do?

'I appreciate where they've come from but it's really very difficult not to lose my rag with those tradesmen.'

'Stop it now! You don't question Mummy. You're not allowed caffeine. You don't question Mummy for the same reason Daddy doesn't.'

'I know it's her culture but blimey blindside I want to punch her in the face sometimes.'

'Hazel, shouting is NOT an option!'

'I love my girls, but sometimes I just want to send them to Asia to learn some manners.'

'Anyone who keeps doing that to their Crocs will NOT be having dim sum at lunchtime. (pause) Felix...' (@MattBaylis2)

'Why is he on the naughty step?' 'Because he kept hitting Mummy's dressing gown with his croissant.' (@RiaSnowdon)

But the finely tuned rules of etiquette must surely be discounted when actual criminal behaviour ensues:

'Once got threatened with removal from Pergamon in Berlin because Scarlett was doing cartwheels (after I suggested it).'

(child about seven years old, being punished) 'That's NOT FAIR! You didn't know about it when I did it. It doesn't count.'

'With triplets the deception can be overwhelming.'

With Holloway Road and its counterfeit cigarette-selling skulkers, we are relieved that the criminal influence on the tots is at a minimum. But being surrounded by the viciously dangerous neighbourhoods of East Finchley, Holloway and (if one falls asleep on the 210 bus) Finsbury Park, it's a relief to know the kids can fight back:

14-year-old daughter to me just now, 'You're being really passive aggressive. That's where I got it from.' (@MichelleLGa)

Five-year-old on bus to friend, 'You're in my personal space.' (@carolinehonour)

Six-year-old on Highgate High Street, lagging behind HM, screaming, 'You are LETTING ME DOWN!'

Toddler in Caffe Nero to his HM, 'I bet your friends HATE YOU.' Couldn't be more than five.

'My child is sulking because she wanted melted goats cheese not raw.' (@squashykat)

Two school boys passing by: '...he said to me, "You can't do anything cos my mum's a lawyer!" So I said, "Tough! Mine is too."' (@CarolinaL0w)

And they'll need all those skills, for there is a tough world beyond the shuddery grubbiness of Tufnell Park:

'Dad, are we allowed to go to South Africa now?'

Kid about five, 'If poor people speak English then they won't be poor and they could be happy.'

'Why is Paris in France? It could be anywhere.' (approx. ten-year-old)

'Why aren't other places like our home?' (future UKIP tot I'm sure)

'He's too young. The closest that child will get to Africa is Sicily.'

That last HM was of course living in a crazy world if she felt she was protecting her kids from the fury of injustice and man's inhumanity to man:

'If I'd wanted a scalp I would have bloody got one. But I took her resignation as an acceptable apology.'

Just heard a very chic woman admonish her scooting toddler with, 'I just don't understand your priorities right now.' (@missellabell)

(to husband) 'Don't talk. Don't crowd me. I've no time and a vital need to fix this issue at the school.'

'Archway's so bloody full of posh mums now that there's no room in any of the cafes to put the pram.'

'The social etiquette for first playdates has obviously changed. She turned up without anything. Not even a shop-bought cake.' (@KjDouglas)

Man on phone outside my son's nursery: 'A shepherd. She's a fucking SHEPHERD! You won't believe who got Mary.' (@mrnickharvey)

'We've had *so* many trips this summer. I'm really stressed out from all the packing.'
(@LouiseRawAuthor)

VERY occasionally, the real world and its trauma crashes and splashes up Highgate West Hill:

'Like everyone, I am appalled by the Islamist attack on Charlie Hebdo. But I am also struck by its similarity to the plot of my last novel.'

Ah, Corbridge. I know someone there whose house was flooded and they were worried about their grand piano.
(@Evie_tweeting)

Nine-year-old: Daddy said there weren't food banks when Labour were in charge. Five-year-old: Is Ed Miliband in charge of Waitrose? (@wotclaire)

Heard on Eurostar, 'Mummy, what does a migrant look like?'

Overheard on the tube at Hampstead by a primary school child, 'I've had enough of that Boris Johnson.' (@NatSasic)

Two posh *Daily Mail* readers fighting with staff at the EasyJet gate. 'But when we went to Cologne last week our case fitted!'

FIRE BRIGADE WARNING AFTER JOSS STICKS FIRE AT KENTISH TOWN FLAT. (@NewJournal)

'Does mental illness exist in children under five? Or is it bad parents? Or are we not allowed to ask that anymore?'

And that concern – albeit bloody insane in places – is very genuine. So this final selection of misguided liberalism was a tough call, and very nearly didn't make it into the book. In defence of my wild HM, do remember that all of the below come from a genuinely kind and well-meaning place:

'I think a black boy going to Oxford is making a very good point to his folks at home and in his neighbourhood.'

'The gym floor is a vanity project. But the community gift of a mural in Wood Green or something would teach them about diversity!'

'Has anyone thought more about my idea to get the nursery kids involved in Calais?' (discussing the Jungle)

'I love, just LOVE Black History Month.'

'Have you thought about how to expand the diversity of Book Group?'

'I don't think it's racist to say that Asians instinctively work hard.'

'Is Empire-Shaming a thing?'

'Eastern European cleaners ARE better. I think they enjoy it more.'

Oh, how I laugh at these daft HM fearing anything beyond the immediate environs of N6. You can feel their stricken fear as someone suggests a trip down Archway's Junction Road.

Er...

But if I'm honest, I do have to remind myself in the twenty-five years I've lived here I have been mugged once. Not in N6, but that very same Junction Road of Fear. So maybe they're onto something after all. Or maybe we should all be a bit better at taking the rough with the smooth and be happy that the house red is rather soothing.

SHOPS & STYLE

'I shop at Sainsbury's. They give money to the Arts. Never at Lidl. They give money to the Germans.'

I'm compiling this chapter in shoes from TK Maxx, trousers from TK Maxx, smalls from Primark. The shirt, I confess, is from Zara, whose Oxford Street church of fabrics intimidated me so. But my colleague Paul helpfully suggested, 'Its cuts work for us larger ladies'.

So the world of fashion, style and retail is bloody alien. Blogger Shannon Ables stated in her podcast, 'Fashion is what you buy. Style is how you wear it.' For me, fashion is what other people buy, and style is pouring Superdrug hand soap into an anonymous container.

So please bear this in mind for this chapter. Ultimately I'm laughing at these HM because I'm jealous as hell:

(HM to teenagers) 'It's nothing if it's not matching. END OF. It's like talking to children with you lot.'

'She's breaking a kaleidoscope of social norms with the curves on her staircase.'

'The Village just isn't a net curtain place. Towards Shepherd's Hill maybe, but not here! It's far too Chinoiserie.'

'Have you seen that exhibition at the Tate? I'm thinking the school reception area should be like that. It gives the less skilled a role.'

Local shop: Free sustainable bamboo knitting needles with skein of organic plant-dyed wool (@Synesthesia) – in Archway too!

(discussing the Amish) 'I love the barn-raising and the simple little life. Not so sure re arranged marriages. How arranged are they?'

'Oh good, now I know what to do with those porcelain glove moulds that are just lying everywhere in my home.'

Remember to work the system out on the high street. Charm and poise, and don't be seen going for the '3 for 2' offers:

Five-year-old girl playing at shops: 'I'll pop in later with my husband's charge card.' (@larkrise2candle)

BANK OF
MA & PA
0123 45678910

(in coffee shop) 'Could you open your heart enough to allow us to treat the Ethiopian blend a day before release?'

'Everything you need is here. Even Ethnic things.'

(to disinterested shop assistant) 'We need this for a party. Have you an idea of its second-hand resale value?'

(to barista in Bear + Wolf) 'When might you be refreshing the toy supplies?'

And the delight of consuming style is blissfully and swiftly appreciated by the tots:

(Near Holloway poundshop) Kid: 'How can nice things be £1?' HM: 'They're not.'

Seven-year-old girl: 'Is Iceland owned by Iceland the country?' HM: 'No. It's just a shop.' Girl: 'Oh right! Like Waitrose.' (@Gilbstar)

'Those pictures are very loud aren't they?' (child about four years old walking past Poundworld window posters)

Kids about six or seven in Le Pain Quotidien playing at shops. 'Have you got the receipt to return this?'

It is never good to encourage mean behaviour, but these bitchy bites really made me choke into my Pellegrino:

'That cut looks fantastic. Which on your skin tone is a surprise.'

'Even though you're on a luxury boat, you're slumming it. The dishwasher is half size and 3G in Portuguese waters is appalling.'

'You can tell his candles are cheap. They're half melted by dessert.'

'Oh, I like your hair. You've stopped dyeing it [to cover the grey]. Now it matches your skin tone.'

With style being such a very personal thing, it's ripe for attack and also in vital need of defence. A well-chosen line can decimate to rubble even the strongest HM psyche. So get those defences up:

'Of course Hampstead's new money, isn't it? It's obvious she'd say something like that.'

'Why attack me? How the child is dressed instructs the teacher how to teach them.'

'A shielded pram is essential, don't you think? You have to protect Baby from the elements, don't you? If it's not flu, it's melanoma.'

'If I keep my sloped roof I'll lose the flexibility, but then again shan't feel so invaded by my neighbour's bush.'

'It's not difficult to say, "I'm X, living in Y and I need planning permission for a Deco fence." It's really not difficult!'

'The problem with the Highgate Society is they resent not living in a house like mine.'

'We are answerable to nothing and nobody except the happiness of the children.'

(discussing the economic slowdown) 'How infuriating! If it's not the plumber it's the texture therapist or bloody £1 an onion at Tesco.'

There is a threat too from within, a fear that one's own failures could let the side down. In these situations it is important to talk about your problems, but always make sure it's done with an air of 'I know this isn't right, but...'

'Why do we suddenly need Japanese-looking shower heads? We've only just installed that bloody eco one.'

'They don't wrap properly at Amazon. At least face-on at Waterstone's you can get them to do it again.'

'Fabric, and fabric appreciation is a skill that we tragically lose as adults.'

'I've been tearing my hair out deciding on a preference colour for the party bags.'

'She's outgrown her John Lewis white baby grows. Thanks to the recession I'll be cutting off the ends and putting her in white socks.'

And gosh, when the faces of the innocent, the future of tomorrow… take a big dump right there on the Java root dining table and humiliate the family name FOREVER:

A mother and daughter shopping in John Lewis, 'no darling, not Molton Brown. It's a bit too high street…'

Lady at the table next to us mocked her son for not knowing the difference between a timber wolf (grey) and Arctic wolf (white). (@Baggsy)

'Westfield is rubbish! Rubbish!! All that space and there isn't even a John Lewis.'

'I said "Don't bring that shit if you're coming from Walthamstow." I used that word. I used "shit", I was that cross.'

'Whatever you say, however you present it, it's a satsuma in all but name.'

Sainsbury's clean out of plain flour and ground ginger. (@W1mum)

'He insists on wearing glasses! I told him he'd have more friends if he wore contacts.'

'SOMEBODY has to be responsible. (sighs) They don't realise the nursery window displays are a front window on OUR CHILDREN!'

'Shall we lunch? Primrose Hill? Oh, but the deli there sells canned goods now.'

Being pretty ignorant on style and the world of retail I've always struggled to understand how the HM psyche works in this area. The HM wants to create a simple air of style that is breezy, but in tandem is sure inform everyone how much effort has gone into it. This ranges from the shop that they saw in Wallpaper magazine ('that nobody knows about yet') to a brand of children's shoes that drives the blood-flow to the brain and promises higher grades as a result.

I write this surrounded by screaming children that are covered in fresh cream. Their HMs chat in perfect unawareness of their kids dashing around the restaurant. And I'm most irritated not by the noise or by the parent's inability to shut down the din by even just the smallest amount, but rather that everyone here – kids included – is dressed better than me.

FINANCE & POVERTY

**Overheard in drinks marquee at Durham graduation:
'Gosh, this is more expensive than Glyndebourne!'**
(@JayneCroghan)

A few years ago, when my salary was a tad more generous than today, I remember imagining a cruel world where I couldn't upgrade my Mac about every eighteen months. 'Why?' I thought to myself, 'wouldn't someone prioritise their spending so as to regularly enjoy that lovely new-Mac smell and feel?'

I don't think any HM overhear from this chapter is quite as appalling as that. And today I'm proud to be writing this book on a battered MacBook Air that I've had for yonks. It has an ALT key that sticks, making it a pain to write a hashtag.

Don't be fooled into thinking the collapse of the world's economy doesn't hit N6 just as hard as anywhere else in the country. Atop the hill, the pain of unemployment can be witnessed first-hand, decimating families, ripping through the self-respect and confidence of men, women and children alike:

Highly perplexed middle-aged couple in Lidl complaining they've no lobster in stock. @dominictlister

'You're not telling me that people don't look and think he's professionally underachieving because she's out working.'

'First thing to say is that New York and Bali are not long enough to be called holidays.'

'The kids have to lose the tertiary playroom. It's a luxury we just can't afford anymore.'

'If it carries on, she will have to forego the pony!' (@xxdy)

My five-year-old burst into tears yesterday when I told her we weren't going to Wagamama for dinner. (@Geebee_H)

'One day, one day I'll be able to put myself first again. (sigh) And sourcing this new au pair is a pain I can do without.'

It's impossible to judge the N6 mood towards poverty and recession. Sometimes there is incredible empathy, sometimes a dazzling failure of thought. But it certainly does sit uneasily on everybody's radar:

'The problem with the Montessori in Archway is the people they have to pass on the way. But the place is fantastic.'

'It might sound trivial, but a housing crisis is a crisis of one's own. And shitty grouting can ruin three new bathrooms. You see?'

Local press headline: Hampstead residents launch 'humanitarian appeal' over Mansion Tax. (@BenjaminRamm)

'I have the school run, flute practice and a personal training session. Who could possibly work and have kids?'

'We're saving money like everyone these days. Egypt hols are now only two weeks and I'm not going to Los Angeles again until February.'

Until February! Goodness knows how long it would be were it not for the brilliant cost-control that the HM have put into place. In their defence, there seems a rather distinct lack of fiscal management from their metropolitan partners. And those who have children tell me that they're a ghastly drain on finances. At least these HM are managing the finances well enough to keep their latte dads in unused gym memberships and to fund their pseudo-macho interest in 'real ale' nights at the local pub:

'It boils down to asking how many times I have to hand over £15k here, £20k there, before demanding some sort of update.'

'We need to decide about how much we can over-max the Princess Party budget without seeking approval from the group.'

'All of us around this table can afford expensive and better if we just work hard enough.'

'If my breakout space has to be another room then so be it. He'll have to make the budget stretch.'

Growing up in lovely suburban semi in Finchley (North London), I used to assume that friends who lived in apartments were either from Paris or had a parent in prison. How come they didn't live in houses? As an adult, I totally don't understand this logic one bit. But it does give me a tinge of guilt to laugh at the next selection:

I heard this loudly in a shop: 'Poor people shouldn't be allowed to have children.' (@PedallingSolo)

Latte Dad on the high street: 'If you have to work 40h a week to earn enough, then you're not getting paid enough.'

'I've never met a hard-working person without a job.'

'If you really want a garden with all your heart, you'll find a way to afford it.'

'Why do the poor eat junk instead of fruit and nuts?'

Apparently I once asked my mum if the people I'd seen on an allotment were peasants. (@UncannyVal)

'Their gardens are so nice you'd never guess they were public housing.'

'How can they really claim poverty when they have a television? Or carpets?'

In N6 there is always some bastard with a bigger house. Rumour is that shirtless world leader Vladimir Putin has turned Witanhurst House into his 'flee-Russia-if-needs-be' pad. How can the HM possibly compete with that?

'Of course you'd never know it to look at them but (looks around, hushed voice) the Chinese are the ones with all the money.'

'She says she has no money, then tells everyone about all the trees she wants to donate to Highgate Woods.'

'There's no money in banking any more. It's all about oil.'
(@KHWorsley)

But a determination to push on through is the hallmark of the HM. A stoicism for the 21st century. Through the pinch they'll find a way to budget, to earn a bit extra, and to fight to keep the N6 flag flying:

'Jasmine loves baby ballet, and it gives me time to work on my interior design business.' (@hayliclifton)

'We hear you. Though we really couldn't live without our fortnightly family trips to the Barbican.' (@WinchesterMummy)

'He says we have to save money and I'm not allowed my "me alone" holiday. But if he can watch football on Sky, I can go to Florence.'

'There's no need to pick up the bill! I was perfectly happy to pick it up the last two times.'

'I don't need job accountability. I've got three children, for God's sake!'

And if nothing else, the financial crash has hopefully fostered a sense of empathy for the less well-off. Well, sort of:

(to child) 'So who are we supporting in the World Cup? Remember it needs to be a poor country. We'll up their spirits!'

'See her playing in the washing basket? She's loving it! There's no way poor children need money for toys.'

'Why are poor children in India always smiling?'

Then again...

'I'm never horrible, I mean I'm not but she needs sacking, pure and simple!' (@RussellMinton)

So is the HM just a spoilt brat, complaining that there aren't the finances to replace the kitchen every three years? If so, I don't think it's deliberate. They just don't know. There is a lot of empathy but it's mixed with genuine confusion:

'He has money to play football on Sundays with his friends, so why can't we afford the long weekend in Jo'burg?'

And whilst subbing this chapter, the space bar of this old laptop has also started to stick a bit. Or at least I'm telling myself that. Because not that far into my psyche I'm thinking that the next book should be written on a nice new machine. The narrative would deserve it. Something that is fresh, bright, light, and has that new-Mac feel and smell...

MUMMY'S VOICE

'She asked why English people don't make coffee in Starbucks. I said because of Tony Blair. I'm so proud that she found it funny.'

An early episode of *Absolutely Fabulous* featured a furious Edina Monsoon in court, filled with rage at the stupidity of people. 'Just have a stupidity tax! Only tax the stupid people!' she screamed. I suspect there were a lot of nodding heads in N6:

'If you don't have a portable chiller she's not even bothering to answer emails.'

'She's a great PA but there's only so far you can go without the love of children. At the very least nieces and nephews.'

'I don't want you thinking I use her sinuses as a get-out-of-jail card.'

'What next? A suggestion to get a builder in from some high street?'

'I'm aware that I can be overbearing. At the next meeting I will take a step back and let the smaller people talk.'

And crikey, in those moments where the HM feels the podium is theirs, the gloves really can come off:

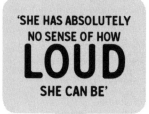

'SHE HAS ABSOLUTELY NO SENSE OF HOW **LOUD** SHE CAN BE'

'She made that laughable mistake of thinking that I was like her.'

'Yes. That's very, very, very nice. (Pause) Personally I would have done it differently.'

'It's some sort of outreach in Crouch End, though God only knows what she hopes to achieve.'

'Her Japanese friend is so mousy I just feel vulgar by even walking through the room.'

In order to control this tsunami of idiocy, the HM must be firm. Some who don't appreciate the difficulties faced may even call them bossy. Pah! Let them try and live at the top of the hill without bearing their teeth. But it is crucial not to be seen to be harsh. After all, you don't want the others bitching once you've popped off to the toilet:

'I would, I would. But whenever I ask her she feels obliged to give an answer.'

'I'm hearing you, but don't expect me to listen.'

'I don't want a suggestion of suggested street names. I want a "yes" or "no" for the one I put forward.'

'A runner looked after them whilst I had an interview. Well I told them. You're the BBC, find childcare if you want to interview me.'

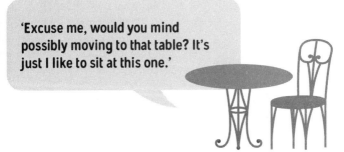

'Excuse me, would you mind possibly moving to that table? It's just I like to sit at this one.'

'It saddens me that in proving myself I had to show the meeting where she'd been going wrong all these years.'

A general must of course earn the trust and faith of their troops. So giving the gang some love, and a sense of inclusion, is absolutely critical:

'That woman will never learn to do exactly what I tell her to.'

'Didn't Charlotte used to run that book publishing company? I'm sure she'd be delighted to manage the photocopying.'

'It's not about being wrong. It's about not being right and allowing that to be valid.'

'A certain type of parent is able to create a momentum behind things like this without having to first ask permission.'

(to group) 'I do like having this "us" time... before Janet arrives at half past.'

'What are we, if not right?'

Much of this book is about the wonder of children, but for the HM and her high standards even these miniature perfections are a pain in the fanny:

'I can feel it when she doesn't validate my scolding.'

(to circa eight-year-old in cafe) 'Can you say in all honesty that your behaviour this morning warrants such a selection?'

'I'm very proud that she's going to study abroad, but how does that benefit anyone left here? Me?'

'Darling. Darling. Darling, LISTEN. Listen. This is time for us to converse. Not just talk. You remember we talked about the difference?'

'I have to remind my girls that their behaviour reflects badly on me. And to some extent their father.'

The HM does strive for a life bursting with fitness, not just for herself but also her family. Vibrant red cheeks are a vital ingredient to successful living atop N6:

Woman in pristine running gear in Southwold. Loudly: 'I only did a super-quick 6k today. I had a ciabatta in the oven.'

(@Smally1969)

'I don't want to be prejudiced but I have to look at them all day. Why would I want a chubby manny?'

'He tried to have sex with me in his tux from the opera. I just laughed and left the room.'

Living is tough. As a former resident myself one of the terrible truths is that commercial rent is too high for independents retailers. So despite its village moniker, the high street is a collection of average coffee shops selling acceptable coffee. But for the exceptional stuff a fearful journey must be taken down the hill to Archway. Beyond those slopes there be dragons...

'If I'm honest I'd never noticed how many trees there were in Archway. Really quite remarkable. You'd think it was here.'

'Oh, God. Oh, God, Oh, God. Euston Road. EUSTON ROAD!'

'To get to the British Museum on public transport is impossible. The logistics involve a change at Euston. Imagine the chaos.'

'I got a migraine after passing those awful people on the South Bank with their skateboards.'

'I've not been to that theatre. Is it mostly a South London audience?'

Hard efforts from the HM are thwarted at every turn by stupidity. Husbands, professionals. All of them under deliver, underachieve and make the whole show a damn shambles:

'My husband puts the washing machine on before work and then I'm bloody distracted in morning yoga and meditation by the noise.'

'Doctors are as bad as teachers.'

'Ha! They make a valiant effort, but it is ultimately just an effort.'

'If they're cheap, fold the sheets and don't steal the leftovers you're onto a winner!'

'... and of course if they're not speaking good English they can't understand my little critiques and criticisms.'

In all the disappointment it's good to hear the other HM's opening up about their pain. Open communication is key to good mental health. And without the ear of a good chum, it's tough to see how they would survive:

'There isn't time to breathe what with the kids back at school in three weeks and the sofa delivering a week Friday.'

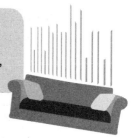

'I'm breaking my bloody head helping their charity and for what in return? I'm being rhetorical, but you see my point?'

'That's brilliant. Really brilliant; the sort of idea I would come up with if I wasn't so tired.'

'Yes, we can sit up here. Or go downstairs where it's nicer... Whatever you prefer. Really. It's your choice.'

'Breakups are always worse on the wife. Because they care.'

'I'm fed up to the back teeth with commuting to that hole outside Dieppe just to manage a bunch of lazy builders tiling the hallway.'

'I've got some telly coming on soon, but really it's nothing to talk about. BBC One don't know what to do with it.'

So dearest HM, keep your head high, keep strong, keep sane. Shape the world around to fit your needs, and yours alone:

'I can co-ordinate fine from France. It's not too inconvenient for you all to work to my time zone, is it? It's only an hour.'

'Is it okay if my son plays behind the till for a bit?'

(to waitress standing by hysterical girl about four years old) 'She's crying because you gave the change to me. Do you mind taking it back and giving it to her?'

'The joy is they can turn any public space into a playroom. And so they should.'

So the imbecilic world, drowning in thudding dim-witted efforts of EVERYONE ELSE clamours its way into the HM lifestyle. Having to roll one's bubble in the grubbiness of the real world must be an ongoing challenge to HM everywhere, from Perth to Brooklyn. But that said, without the Other against which to compare lives and behaviour, the HM has no definition at all. And that would NEVER do.

LATTE DADS

'She's going to Vietnam. But the nice parts. The ones that are like Asia. Still 'Nam, though.'

Before we reach the end of this book, let's not forget that HMs are not aren't restricted gender. Let's talk about the latte dads.

The latte dads are wonderful, magical creatures. In a world that is generally dominated by women, they're a sparkling species all their own. They're beautifully sensitive and metrosexual, whilst simultaneously seduced by a desire to reclaim their masculinity. They think they're in army games, when it's actually just a suburban edition of *It's A Knockout*:

'I'm a broken man walking up that hill two or three times EVERY DAY.' (Highgate Hill – to be fair – is quite a trek up from Archway)

'The barber's electric razor really struggles with my thick stubble.'

'She's complaining that my kit stinks. But I'm like, "Hey, it's just man smell."'

'The stag weekend'll be blinding awesome, mate. Before tipping the beers we've got a private thing at Museum Montanelli.'

Chelsea yoga studio – Man: the Saracens game started at three, but I didn't want to know the result before yoga.
(@williamtfox)

The men do tend to bunch in groups, finding safety in each other's battles. There's a lot of gasping at a testosterone battle on Parliament Hill Fields or an impressively swift stroke at the ridiculously shallow Archway leisure pool. And swearing it seems is the key to driving home the vital masculinity of the moment:

'I'm fucking furious with myself for missing the deals at Keela.'

'I gashed my finger putting it up. There was literally blood on the rug. Fucking LITERALLY.'

'It's a crushing BOLLOCK of an experience parking up at the school.'

'The food options for kids at the Emirates Stadium are a SHITTING mess.'

Just heard on Tottenham Court Road, 'Rosé wine's so fucking overrated, man.'

'I'm going to neck me a FUCK load of caffeine.'

'All you need are some fucks and those cartoons would be like Tarantino movies. It's awesome.'

And let's not forget that these latte dads live just as much under the influence of the HM. Just like their children in school, the latte dad is expected to excel, over-perform, and above all deliver:

'Just because I'm excited doesn't mean I'm satisfied, or indeed happy about it. I had to point that out to him.'

'Children need clear identities. I never apologise to my husband in front of the children. It would confuse them.'

'Life is life. And I don't care what my husband says, I won't let his redundancy get in the way of skiing. Don't I deserve it?'

'He's QUITE happy to leave the responsibility of teaching to the school. I'm aghast. Yes, AGHAST.'

'We should employ our husbands as PAs. Then they might realise how busy we are!'

'I've nothing to say about his obsession with this Freecycle site. Nothing AT ALL.'

'Refusing an in-laws invite as it states "Harvester or Beefeater" as the venue. Husband thinks I'm being too HM.'
(@EmilyFlump)

'I went on the Northern Line the other day to go into town for lunch. I don't know what my husband complains about. Commuting seems easy.'

'It impresses nobody knowing Stradavarius and Cohiba Esplendido cost a bomb.'

And, hell, the men are even tough on each other:

(to circa five-year-old) 'You need to cut your hair, little man. You look like a revolutionary!'

Just now overheard in Tesco: 'There's a weakness in a man who takes the sweetness of a fortified wine.'

'I reckon you can count on one hand the number of times he can lift his own body weight.'

'He's incredibly camp and knows less than zero about Galliano.'

And with such hulking bodies to carry about, it's little wonder that there's not necessarily a lot of brain space left for practicalities. Sometimes it seems as if life would be so much easier if the latte dad were to stay locked in his man cave:

Four-year-old, from lounge 'Help!!! I'm stuck in Daddy's yoga mat.' (@rebeccajohns)

Latte Dad squirming a bit in his seat, friend asks what's wrong. Answer, 'I don't know. I think these might be my wife's running shorts.'

'I admire single mums, I really do. But if I'm honest how much help do my husband and au pair really provide? Answer? Not much!'

But the love of a latte dad is without question, albeit delivered in a way that feels as if the HM is the puppeteer…

Father to four(ish)–year-old son on Tube train, 'Calm down, use your yoga breathing.' (@intl_jane)

'Hurry up, let's do the Roman stretches before your tennis.'

But despite his swearing, the foul-smelling gym kit and a mud-smeared (often quite sexy) dad-bod, these hairy residents of N6 can have a taste just as refined as kids and HM:

'You've got to have the sweetened one, dude. The unsweetened stuff tastes like cum smells.' (discussion about soya milk)

'You've got to be kind to your hands if you're going to be lifting weights.'

'**This shower curtain is so naff, I've never seen the likes, that's the last time I stray from John Lewis.**' (@AbigailHazrati)

Can't believe I just had to ring husband from middle of Waitrose and ask if he minds if pork chops are not organic. (@katewatsonsmyth)

Considering most of this book has been written under caffeine, I absolutely loved this blinder from what I think was a med student from the nearby Whittington Hospital:

'**No footie for me this week, dude. I got to hit the cafes if I'm going to prepare for this exam.**'

The greatest gift of the latte dad is that he proves the HM has absolutely nothing to do with gender. The horrors of middle-class fear are just as much his provision as of the HM. A good latte dad overhear is relatively rare because there simply aren't that many dads in the cafes of N6 and N19. It would be fantastic to collect far more of these. The HM rarely feel any threat to their femininity and so the latte dad trying to weave his masculinity into the mix is fascinatingly unique. The poor chap curses and Tough Mudders to feed the defiant teen within, but can only blanche as he looks up and faces the crushing realities of adulthood.

ARMY OF EARS

My HM moment was my then four-year-old's: 'Mummy your teeth are the colour of Camembert.' Cringed and bought extra whitening toothpaste. (@liathughesjoshi)

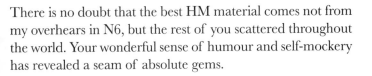

There is no doubt that the best HM material comes not from my overhears in N6, but the rest of you scattered throughout the world. Your wonderful sense of humour and self-mockery has revealed a seam of absolute gems.

So, this final chapter is dedicated to those who follow the account on social media. The exhausted HM who find the time and energy to log into Twitter, Facebook or email me gets a big round of applause. For this eye-rolling introspection is what HM is turning into. And will be all the better for it!

I've stored a number as 'acupuncture' in my phone. Not sure if it's for mine or the cat? Coming over all HM. (@EmilyFlump)

Feeling a bit HM all the way from Scotland having to feed the ducks wholemeal pitta bread from M&S. (@kellydowmcghee)

Tragic story heard in the west end of Glasgow; the dog is allergic to incense. (@loomagooo)

Missy won't eat non-organic meat. She loves corn fed chicken. Never mind HM, we need @highgatecats. (@tomslominski)

The overhears about discipline are the ones that I'm often accused of making up. So it's good to know that other people hear things that are beyond what I could ever have imagined:

I overheard a mother say, 'If you don't start behaving there'll be no trip to the library.' Stern words indeed. (@mcbiiig)

On train in Scotland. 'No darling, no juice. It's a Pavlovian response with you, isn't it.' (@Amprsndcstls)

At soft play, overheard a child tell his mum, 'He was mean so I 'it him.' 'Hit.' Enunciated Mum (@Cyberturnip)

I just admonished the dog with the immortal line, 'Audrey, do not embarrass me. In Hampstead, of all places.' (@Sarahthoms14)

Just heard a mum tell a toddler he was 'clearly overstimulated and needed to focus on the task at hand'. (@postscriptwords)

We've already covered education, but these couple of gems deserve their own space:

Today, I had a grown-up rant on Facebook over the ridiculous reward system at eight-year-old / five-year-old's school. WHAT HAVE I BECOME? (@Twitflup)

In daughter's primary school, they are put in groups Papaya, Mango, Avocado whatever happened to Red, Blue, Green. (@DianaBo)

Contrary to expectations, lifestyle seems not to be something that is actively sought. It's just there. A bit like a good waiter:

Slight HM dilemma about whether to use the 'good' olive oil on the baby's dry skin. (@Dr_RaulDuke)

At the kids playground at Kew Gardens. It's basically Highgate Mums: The Movie. (@EmilyofTours)

Five-year-old overheard, 'We've got so many flowers mummy has had to put some of them in a carafe.' (@HelenStead2)

(in Richmond) 'Well, we went to Center Parcs but that isn't really a holiday is it?' (@LawrenceJunior)

My own daughter – oh, the shame... 'Mum, you know the marshmallow challenge? We should do the biscotti challenge!' (@anenglishmum)

Swimming with my three-year-old yesterday near the pool pump: 'Mummy it feels just like the hot tub.' (@StaceyTatham)

Yesterday in my singing class a ten-year-old said, 'I wish I was at the Spa.' (@nhagc)

Feeling very HM this morning, the children are playing croquet. Indoors. (@Ruth_E_Chapman)

And there's plenty of cases where proper posh has dazzled you:

The 'homework' in the Primrose Hill pregnancy yoga class: Buy yourself something in cashmere this week.' (@lrohde)

Overheard today, 'They live in *Clapham*, it may as well be Belgium.' (@50shadesoftrace)

A kid at my kid's school is giving up croissants for lent. (@bronwynnortje)

And talking of food...

I just got caught dipping my finger in the watercress pesto. (@TrippyPip)

Middle-class quote of the day: 'Watercress is out of season? Wankers.' (@RufusHound)

Overheard at a hip noodle bar in WC1, 'Oh no! I forgot to bring Sarah-May's little chopsticks.' (@evvvvil)

A friend just told me that her seven-year-old daughter recently went to a birthday party catered only with sushi.
(@mitfordian)

Outside Selfridges, 'Excuse me, your little boy is about to drop his orange.' Frosty reply, 'It's a clementine.'
(@Sparklyboy1)

I just typed the phrase 'and can you believe they have no Iranian saffron?' In reference to my local Morrisons. Help me... (@amanandapencil)

The teens in your house seem to cause rather a lot of amusement too. As a childless spinster I assumed it was only the tots who could be HM, as the teens would reject poshness for rebellion. How wrong I was:

'I'm ashamed to say the daughter was worthy of HM prior to uni, 'How will I manage without longhorn mince?' (@oedipusscat)

Overheard at Oxford Uni: 'What did you do this summer?' 'Oh not much, I only went to Peru.' (@LizCBraithwaite)

Someone has written their name in the cement on Highgate's Southwood Lane. Of course it's Highgate so it says 'Lucia'.

And the Arts continue to play an important role:

'She has to watch *I'm a Celebrity* to be able to talk to the other girls the next day. We wouldn't have it on otherwise.' (@larkrise2candle)

My six-year-old niece has just told me she enjoys the paintings of Georges Seurat. (@ReetuKabra)

'Nathan, please go around the house and gather up ALL the music stands. Not the wooden one, OBVIOUSLY.' (@annemariewyley)

And there's some lovely stuff that doesn't really fit under any category:

Very posh rugby mum in Cardiff last night: 'Bethany, they must be football fans, they don't know how to behave at a rugby match.' (@JimboFB)

At Highgate tube station today someone had written 'misplaced apostrophe' beside a notice with a misplaced apostrophe. (@meadowgroove)

Here in Hereford, I saw 'Sebastian has a small penis' in tiny teen calligraphy at the playground. (@JudSawyer)

Our final block has to be dedicated to the kids, the very reason the HM exist at all. Marvel. They shall inherit the Earth. And the Aga.

Just had a HM moment at a kid's party quiz: 'What type of cake do you eat at Xmas?' My kid's answer: panettone. (@rebecca_hardy)

My eight-year-old daughter told me that she couldn't sleep because, 'I can't find my inner peace.' I give up. (@Gasprey)

Eight-year-old on passing allotments, 'Look daddy, it's a favela!' (he lives in Crouch End). (@williamtfox)

Six-year-old wrote a general knowledge quiz. It included a question on Pointillism. (@wotclaire)

Three-year-old daughter pointed to a picture of a mouse in a book and said, 'Look mummy — vermin.' (@katecusack)

Six-year-old getting onto a bus in Crouch End: 'Ooh la la, isn't this nice!'

My four-year-old niece to my four-year-old daughter, 'So, how are things going at school?' (@rulitos14)

Three-year-old bends backwards and exclaims, 'I'm doing the Sun Salutation pose!' I fear we've gone a bit HM. (@becb1984)

And how to end a patchwork book like this? There always was ever only one choice. Overheard by me at Côte Brasserie on Highgate High Street about two years after the account had been created. This was when I first realised that the account was becoming more than just a bunch of friends following my tweets. Even better it showed me that the HM were a bunch of sassy people with the wit and intelligence to laugh at themselves.

So drumroll, and big applause to this HM. If you know who you are, drop me a line. You deserve a bottle of bubbles!

'I'll end up on Highgate Mums one day.'

ABOUT THE AUTHOR

Dan Hall has been running the @Highgatemums Twitter account since 2012. He lives in London.